MESSAGES FROM MATHIAS

Messages of Love, Hope, and Encouragement for the Coming Changes

channeled by
Robin James

Messages from Mathias

Wellstone Publications
295 East Main
Ashland, Oregon 97520

ISBN 0-9647066-8-7

Cover art by Jeremiah Jones
Interior art by Jochen Ziems

First printing September 1997

Printed in the United States of America

WELLSTONE PUBLICATIONS

CONTENTS

Foreword

In the spring of 1991, I was told that a new guide named Mathias was present with me and that he was available for automatic writing. The following messages from Mathias were channeled through me.

It became apparent to me during this work that these messages were not meant for me alone. I have deleted only the most personal comments.

I want to thank Mel, Karla, and my husband Scott for their assistance and support in this work, and especially Joshua, who introduced me to Mathias.

Robin

I

THE CALL

*F*or many will benefit as a result of your willingness to be as a light in the darkness. This darkness is man's separation from his true spirit, his true oneness with God. It is all a matter of acceptance, faith, and joy. Joy is our true nature.

The opportunities are boundless, boundless if one only has faith in God and in himself. For within lies all Love, all light, which is needed for all things. We are truly unlimited. Each soul accepts exactly what it is ready to accept in its spiritual growth and development. The more workers, the greater and more swiftly comes the light, moving the Earth's consciousness ahead into what it is meant to be — one of joy, Love, sharing, growth, and much potential.

The Earth will evolve into a much healthier, more beautiful existence. Pain, fear, and guilt will be overcome with the help of those willing to serve as a beacon, to guide others through the darkness onto the one true path, the path of Love.

Shalom

II

THE PATH
OF LOVE

oday we speak of many things — of joy, of Love, of peace. This world is unfolding exactly as it should. Every injustice, every suffering has its purpose. For through these things, man has chosen to learn many lessons. There is justice in the world if one sees through His eyes, His Love. It may not appear so, but it *is* so.

Now why do so many souls require pain and suffering in their lives? It is because they have forgotten the way of Love. These lessons need not be learned in this manner, but the individuals have chosen so. Their separation, their fear demand that they learn in this manner. As they progress, this will change. There are easier ways, more loving lessons to be learned and experienced.

Choose Love and that Love shall set you free. Freedom is something that very few beings truly understand, truly accept. They yearn for freedom, and yet they know not how to choose freedom. They choose fear and pain. The way to freedom is through Love and sharing this Love. The way to pain is through fear and spreading that fear.

There was a man who came to Earth to teach the ways of Love, of freedom. That man's name, of course, was Jesus. What matters is that one knows the essence of His being, His Love. By knowing this Love and expressing it in this world, shall ye be free. This freedom is everlasting. Set forth on the path of Love; for it is this path which leads to oneness with God, that destiny which is the *only* destiny of each and every soul on this Earth, in all of existence.

It is a great plan, a diverse, multifaceted existence, little of which is understood on your plane. But that matters not. For the essence of all that is, is all that matters, and that is Love. Love shall set you free. It shall build mountains, ford streams, shine great joy upon each and every sadness and grief in so many hearts. Love is the way, the only way. Sharing Love is the greatest gift one can give another. If all truly shared the Love in their hearts, this world would be a great light in the skies, a radiating planet of joy and rebirth.

The times ahead are designed to develop that sense of Love, to reopen hearts to the knowledge of this Love. For all shall one day know God. Their paths are arduous, it seems, but all shall meet their destiny. All shall be enfolded in His arms once again. With your help and others like you, working in the light, we shall make this Earth a place of pleasure, not pain — Love, not fear — life, not death.

Walk the path as a lantern, lighting the way for so many others. We realize this path shall not always be easy for you, but the rewards will be great; and we will be here with you always, sharing your joys, your successes, your disappointments. Let not those disappointments deter you or impede your faith in any way. For great joy shall be yours for your efforts.

Reinforce that Love that you feel, that you experience, by sharing it with others. This is the path of enlightenment. More and more will see this, grow to really know this in their hearts; and slowly but surely, every corner of the world will grow in brightness, in joy, and in Love. Sweetness and light shall reign once again in the hearts of many, and true Love will make itself known in so many ways.

Shalom

III

COME
TOGETHER

estraining yourself is not the answer, the answer to working for and in the light. His message must be spread far and near, loud and clear. For how else will His children come together in Love and unity? The words will echo 'round the Earth in praise of His ways, His Love. The result will be peace, hope, and joy in the hearts of one and all. The result will be the rebirth of light and hope in the hearts of everyone. No one will be exempt from this blessing.

Times are changing. The changes are occurring now. The time of freedom is at hand. Rapidly approaching is that hour when all must join together to proclaim their Love for our Father-Mother God. Restrain yourself no more. For now is the time to come forward, to come together in peace and in this common work, bringing all His children together in the name of Love. For Love conquers all — all fears, all sadness, and misunderstanding.

The way has not been clear for so many. But this is

about to change, is changing as we speak. Love, justice, and joy in living are about to make themselves known in the hearts of so many who have been living in fear, in pain — in fear of claiming their rightful heritage, that of oneness and of Love. Receive the blessings which abound, which are available for all if they will but open their hearts and let them in. All it takes is acceptance and faith. Follow your heart and release the fear that has been holding you back, keeping you from experiencing the joy that is to be found in devotion to the way of Love and of faith.

Faith is the key which will open many hearts, faith that all is perfect now and forevermore. Once that is accepted, the possibilities are endless — the possibilities for true peace on this planet. Peace must start in each and every heart. For what we see about us is what is manifested from within our hearts. True peace starts within. Receive the blessings of peace through knowing His Love within, and the whole world will benefit from this knowledge, this Love. The whole world will reflect the Love which is felt within.

Strange, isn't it, that it is thought that guns and killing will bring peace? Nothing is further from the truth. Violence begets violence. Cruelty begets cruelty. The only true path is through Love, faith, and knowledge that we are all one. Look at each man, woman, or child as your own brother, sister, or child. Love that person as you love your own family. Accept every individual just as they are, seeing them as the perfect reflection of God's Love that they truly are if they would but accept. As *you* accept it, *they* will begin to accept. And the light of wisdom will grow within their hearts until they truly recognize themselves at one with all and with God.

And don't forget the one who truly needs and deserves your Love — YOU. For you are a precious child of God to be honored, loved, and respected in every action, deed, and thought. Love begins at home, within the self. From there it radiates out to the rest of the world, to all your brothers and sisters. Join hands with all those around you, and you will feel the joy of unity, peace, and prosperity. For where many join together in His name, the light will be brightest. Resume old habits, and the darkness will be perpetuated.

Begin this day as a new day in brotherhood with all you meet. Truly open your hearts and release the fear which has been limiting your Love, your potential, your ability to truly see your brothers and sisters as a part of thee, a part of all in Love and acceptance. He will rejoice as He sees His children holding hands, sharing their Love in His name. For this is what we are here to do — to open up to true Love, the only Love there is.

His Love, His joy, His peace shall be known in the hearts of those who open up to love themselves and their brothers and sisters. Peace shall reign on this Earth once more. All shall be under His wing, guided, protected, and shown the way. Great joy will be felt in the hearts of those who accept His Love through acceptance of themselves and the Love that is being offered to them.

Just around the corner is great change for many, events that will challenge many, enlighten many, events that are meant to separate those who would choose Love from those who will choose fear and perish in that fear. You are being called to accept these challenges in Love and in faith — the faith that through Him and His Love, all is possible.

The way will become clear to those who respond to His call. All those who do will begin working together, working together for and in the light. And the world which so many have yearned for will become reality — a world filled with peace, good cheer, good will, and justice for all.

Love shall light the way for all those who have found themselves in darkness along the path. Their brothers and sisters will take their hands and lead them through the darkness into the light — the light of brotherhood, peace, and sharing the knowledge that we are all one.

Shalom

IV

CO-CREATORS

oday as we speak, those changes which shall enlighten the Earth are taking place. His children are realizing that their ways of fear no longer serve. For many are experiencing the results of lifetimes of habit, of fear. As never before, they are being shown the error of their ways and the hope that lies ahead if they will but listen to their hearts, follow their hearts in joy and in Love. For what awaits those who are true to themselves and their light is such perfect joy, such light, that they cannot help but choose this path once they know the promise of what lies ahead if they do.

A return to the true path is what is occurring. This path is Love. You have heard this, we have said this. It has been said by many over and over. But how to apply this in your life? By feeling that Love and by expressing it. No longer hide your feelings, your joy, within your heart for fear of being misunderstood, ridiculed. Come forth into the light with your truth, your faith. The rewards will be great. Act out of Love, not fear. Release the fetters which have been binding your heart, holding you back from expressing what you truly know and feel. As you do this, you will encourage others to do the same.

Resounding within your heart is the courage to do so. All that you require for all things is provided by your Higher Selves, your guides, your God. Fear not the consequences of truth. For in truth lies the key to freedom — truth, faith, and Love. The dam breaks, and Love pours forth as you release the fear that has been trapped in your heart for so long. Fear hath no place in the new world, the new consciousness which is about to emerge.

All things are perfect. Knowing this, how can there be any fear? God watches over each and every soul. As they request His help, He hears and answers their prayers in joy and in Love. So sweep clean the past. Begin anew in the knowledge that as a child of God, Love, joy, and hope are your true heritage, your true destiny.

Formulate the questions in your mind. Send them forth to Him, and they will be answered, clearly and concisely. You have just to listen and have faith that the answers are from Him in all His wisdom and Love. He shall show you the way to true joy and fulfillment.

Great movement is taking place within the hearts of man. He is ready to be led, ready to believe that all is not a big cosmic joke, but a plan of perfection. Hearts will fill with joy as this truth becomes known. Great deeds will be accomplished with the new hope that fills everyone's heart. For there has been a great longing on this planet for a sense of unity, a sense of purpose. The time has come for His purposes to unfold, to become known to all. So many are lost, wandering, wondering why they are here. "For what?" they ask. "Is this all there is — this facade of emptiness, of joylessness, of unkindness, of lack of purpose?"

A facade it is. The truth has been hidden from their hearts through fear — fear of claiming their rightful heritage, fear of self-Love and expressing that Love to the world around them. What greater purpose on this Earth than Love? This is what we long for — to be enfolded in loving, caring arms. We are all so enfolded if we will but accept and acknowledge this Love. Each heart must get in touch with this Love that is offered, get in touch with the Love within and express it to themselves, first and foremost. This Love can create the world we are all longing for.

We must accept our power as co-creators with God. For in truth, we have created this world, and we have the power to *uncreate* it — to uncreate the fear, the pain, the suffering. All it takes is courage, truth, conviction, the intent, and Love. If enough souls agree upon the changes, they will become reality. Now is the time to join together to create the new world for which we long — one where peace, truth, commitment, and Love abound. As these things abound in our hearts, so will they be created as a manifestation without, in the Earth.

Call now upon the truth in your heart to change those habits, those fears, which have been blocking your ability to truly serve as a channel of Love and of truth in this world. Call upon your guides, your God, to come to your aid to effect these changes as rapidly as possible. For there is much work to be done, many hearts to be enlightened with joy and with hope of a new and better world. The purpose of Life is unfoldment — unfoldment of His Love, His perfection.

The purpose of life is to end the separation from God that man has imposed upon himself for so very long, to become aware of the one true source of all, and to be rejoined in oneness, in purity of Love and purpose.

Hold hands now as we experience the rebirth of light together. As we share the joy ahead together, all things are possible, all things are probable. Led by Love, faith, and belief in God, we shall overcome lifetimes and lifetimes of fear, of pain, and of darkness. Realizing that this is our purpose shall make the work much easier, the goal reached much more quickly.

The time is upon us for His return to the consciousness of the Earth, where every heart will know of His presence, His Love. And every hand will reach out to grasp the hands of their brothers and sisters in Love and in assistance of making reality the purpose of becoming at one with each other, with Him. His consciousness, His Love, shall reign upon the Earth for 1000 years. Your job is to help bring that consciousness to as many hearts and minds as is possible. For we shall all join together in light, in Love, and in hope. And this world, this Earth, shall outshine the brightest star as His Love radiates to every heart — enlightening, loving, and healing every soul who shall heed His call.

We are present in this work. We encourage each and every one of you to call forth your Higher Selves, your angels and guides, in assistance for the purpose of showing you the way more rapidly, more clearly. For there is much work to be done: mountains to be moved, hearts to be freed, souls to be saved — saved from fear and lack of self-Love, saved from self-pity. This is not the way to freedom.

The way to freedom, peace, and Love evermore is giving up those old habits of self-incrimination, self-flagellation, and accepting self in Love, seeing and knowing the true beauty that shines within self and within each soul. It is accepting that Love and letting it pour forth from within your heart to reach out to your brother, to your sister, to become one with all in Love, hope, and charity.

In this way shall peace reign once again upon this Earth, and He shall look with eyes of Love and praise for His children upon the Earth. He is calling you now. Answer His call now, and forever have all doubt, all fear, all pain removed from your consciousness. This is His wish for you. This is His hope and His joy.

Shalom

V

TRUST IN SELF

rust in yourself. For no one knows better than you the truth within. All action should be based upon this truth, this knowledge that is within your heart. By always following this truth, all paths shall be clear, all action correct. For trust in self is at the basis of self-Love.

Remaining within the confines of what others expect of you is limiting, denying your own power and faith. Release yourself from the expectations of others, and you shall know the freedom of faith in God and faith in self. For shall you serve the wishes of others or follow faithfully the truth and Love within thine own heart?

So many do not trust the knowledge within their hearts. Here is all the knowledge that ever need be known. Have faith in self and this truth which is within your heart. Be guided by those whom you love and trust, but ultimately all answers lie within thine own heart. Rejoice in the fact that you are all-knowing. You have but to accept this fact, and the path shall be clear. We do not trust ourselves. Have faith in self and in God, for He knows all things and shall reveal to you all truth that is needed on your path of enlightenment.

And judge not what is truth for another person. For each must find his own way, that which is best for him and no other. Have total faith in the knowledge within and judge not the paths of others, supporting and encouraging others on their paths, whatever they may be. For the light will be manifested within many in different ways.

We are each unique in our way, in our Love. God has planned it that way: that each soul shall be a creator in his own right, to be guided and loved by Him, but nonetheless a co-creator with freedom to choose his own path. Of course, all paths lead to attunement, to oneness with Him. And many choose many diversions along the way. But that is their choice, their right.

Ask for His help along your path, and He will be there — ever watchful, ever loving, ever accepting. Return to the path of Love is His wish for all, but all paths are honored and given equal acceptance. Release yourself from self-incrimination, self-judgment, and do the same for your brothers and sisters.

We are all traveling along the same path. The illusion is that we are separate. Choose to judge your fellow man, and you will be judged. Treat others harshly, and you will experience that treatment. Love self truly, honestly, and fully, and you will experience that Love from others.

Somewhere along the way, you will be asked to choose between self-gratification and service to God. The choice is yours, the decision unjudged. Know that choice is yours. Freedom awaits you at the end of the tunnel, no matter what your choices now.

You may facilitate your path, or you may make it arduous, with many pitfalls and delays. But all shall one day come before Him in Love, in light, and in joy. The way shall become more passable through your acceptance of self and all others in Love, without judgment, and in the truth that we are all one — all here to love one another, help each other in any way possible.

"Judge not lest ye be judged." Let that be your motto. Let that guide your dealings with those whom you meet along the way. Give unconditionally, with Love in your heart and the knowledge that each is a part of you, struggling to open himself to accept God's Love and wisdom.

Comfort your brothers and sisters, for they need comforting. Encourage them, for they need encouragement. Speak your truth to them, for they need to hear the truth. Their ears are willing, yearning to hear the truth. Be not afraid. But speak out from the heart willingly, gladly, knowing that you are helping many in your bravery, your openness, and willingness.

All hearts shall be as one, sharing common Love, knowledge, and joy under His wing, His guidance.

So shall the new world be born — born in Love, out of Love that we acknowledge and share — in joy, out of the joy that we express and accept — out of faith, that faith that He is with us, guiding us always in the ways of truth and Love. And we shall become like children once again — our spirits free and playful, innocent and loving, trusting and at peace.

Shout your Love, and you will be heard. Others will want to share your Love and abandon. Be not afraid. For it is time to release the fear, the guilt, the anger that has existed so long within our hearts, our minds.

Begin each day mentally releasing all guilt, all pain, all fear. Let it be known to God, to self, that you are now ready for a new life where Love, joy, freedom, and faith will fill the void where fear, guilt, and anger once lived within your hearts. These things have no place in the new world, the new consciousness which is emerging. Release these dark feelings into the light, making room for freedom.

Wait not another day. For now is the time to truly become at one with all of life, with your God. Restrain yourself no more. For great joy shall follow your determination to begin anew in acceptance and in Love. Releasing old habits, all fears, will fill your heart with lightness and joy you thought not possible. The results will be so incredible, so beautiful, so enlightening, that you will want to share it with others. Do so, for it is in this sharing that others will be encouraged and supported to do the same.

We are here to change this world. You have chosen this time to enter the Earth to work for and in the light. The time is upon us, and we must begin within. Make a clean sweep within your heart and begin to experience what we have come to experience — Love, joy, and hope of a brighter tomorrow.

That tomorrow is today. There is no future, no past, only the now. Choose to do these things now, and peace will begin to reign upon this Earth. As each soul opens up to his potential, his truth, his beauty, things will change — slowly for some, quickly for others. It is all a matter of perspective. But change they will, and you can be a part of that change through accepting God, His Love, His hope, His faith.

In each daily occurrence there is opportunity — opportunity to choose Love over fear, faith over fear, joy over guilt. Choose the path your heart speaks to you. You will know it, you will feel it. And you will rejoice in the rewards of choosing Love over fear and faith over reason.

For your minds would have you believe it is not "reasonable" to have hope of a new world emerging, to have faith that God is within one and all. Our minds play tricks, but our hearts know the truth — the truth of His Love, His light. That light is within your own heart. You are an extension, a part of all He is. You can be all that He is, in truth, if you will but accept and have the faith to follow that light within.

For joy and Love abound where the heart is allowed to express the Love and the truth within, without the fear of failure, of judgment, of guilt. Give yourself that freedom and then extend that encouragement, that freedom, to all those you meet. Look at them with eyes of Love and compassion, without judgment and without fear. And see the truth that they are your mirror, simply a part of you expressed in a different way, but as deserving of your Love, your respect, as the light within thee.

Go forth meeting everyone as thy equal, for in truth we are all one. This truth shall become known; and all shall be accepted as a part of Him, as a part of self — in Love, joy, and the brilliant light that is uncovered where many hearts are gathered in His name, supporting and encouraging the one true path, that of Love.

Shalom

VI

LOVE

oday we shall speak of Love, not the kind of love one knows from the movies, but true Love which comes from honoring God and living life honoring His tenets. Why do so many hearts reject what they truly feel inside? Why have we chosen to leave the joy of His Love, ignoring all that could be ours in favor of a path of fear?

Man has forgotten his true heritage of oneness and Love of our Father. The world was created to be an experiment in Love and joy. Somewhere along the way, man became lost, separated from his God. The evidence is all around you. The truth has been forgotten in so many hearts.

How to remember the true path? Through intent — intent to begin life anew, to take advantage of the Love and truth that surround us if we would but see. Journey from thy door and meet that evidence of separation. It is all around us. Determine this day to turn this around, not only for yourself, but for your brothers and sisters. See through eyes of Love. The mystery of life is not a mystery at all. The truth is there for everyone to see if they will but open their eyes to truth and to light.

Achieving material success is not the answer. Material success may bring temporary satisfaction, temporary joy. But the joy soon turns to disillusionment as the joy fades, a facade of true happiness. It lies not in romantic love, that attraction on the physical level which brings two people together seeking to complete their incomplete natures, their desire to love and be loved. Remove need and desire from your heart. The only true need, true desire, is knowing and living His Love.

His Love differs from what most consider Love. Passion, true passion, may be found through loving self and God. Why are so many hearts lost? Because they have not been followed, because they have not been listened to. Truly listening to your heart and then following in faith and in joy exactly what it is saying is the key to self-Love and true joy.

Jesus was an example of the miracles which abound when one truly follows his heart. There is no limit to what can be achieved through faith and Love of God and listening to the heart. Shall we begin now to follow the example that has been given to us in Love and in faith? Or shall we continue to close our eyes, our spiritual eyes, to the truth within and the truth which is all about us?

You are deserving of every joy, of every good that you experience. Believe this, and you will begin to understand true Love — His Love for and through you. Feel this Love within your heart for self, and then you can truly express this Love to others. For God created man out of Love, in His image, as His co-creator. Many got lost along the way and forgot their true natures. But this can be changed, will be changed, as we realize that our current lives, our current thoughts and beliefs no longer serve, are dead ends — dead ends upon the road, the journey back to wholeness, wellness, and joy.

Great upheaval must be experienced by many before they accept the fact that change is truly needed, that they have lost the way. For as co-creators, man became greedy for power, lost to the true meaning of creation and the power with which he had been blessed. But this is about to change. God is stepping in, encouraging His beautiful children to go deep within their hearts to remember their true roots, their true purpose — that of oneness, unity, and Love.

"For God so loved the world that He gave His only begotten Son." So that this was not in vain, He is calling His children together once more, aided by His armies of angels, guides, and loving souls whose purpose is to bring enlightenment into our hearts and minds once again, to awaken man's spirit to the truth that all is not lost, that Love shall once again make itself known to those who are willing to open their hearts and minds to allow His spirit to fill the void, the emptiness, the lack of Love in their lives.

Shall you be among those who will hear the call?

Let us hope so. For now, as never before, the opportunities are being presented. The time is now. God's consciousness shall reign once more upon the Earth, shall fill the hearts of man with Love, with joy, with his true desire for oneness and peace.

Release the tensions, the pains, the hurts of the past. Come forward in faith and the knowledge that all lies before thee if ye will but heed His call — His call to Love, to wholeness, to oneness. For all are presented the opportunity, at this time, of God's grace to descend upon them, to help them transcend many lifetimes of being lost to their true natures.

Grace is a gift from God, that gift that will allow us to join together remembering our heritage, our true path. Release the fear that is holding you back. Fear not the loss of identity. For identity is only enhanced through unity, through oneness. Our true identity is found through Him, through accepting His grace in Love and complete trust.

For what shall be lost — our wealth, our sense of superiority? True wealth lies not in any material thing without. True wealth is being in touch with the joy, the Love within that can uplift many in their quest for the light. Superiority to what, to your fellow man? How can one be superior if we are all one? These feelings of superiority are false — false, supported by the separation of man from his true nature, his God.

Believing in self is important in the path of regaining the knowledge, the oneness which we have forgotten. Join with me now with this as our intent, our goal, and He shall guide us along the way in joy, in Love. The opportunities are here each and every day to follow our hearts, to do what we are led to do in truth and in honesty.

Forward is the only way to go. Remaining in the habits of past which no longer serve must be overcome. Rally self, rally your friends and loved ones, to become once again as little children filled with enthusiasm, hope, and joy in the new path which shall lead to completeness and wholeness.

His gifts are always offered. His gift of grace shall light the path. Join with me now as we take the first steps together to enlighten our world, to clasp hands with those around us in our quest for true brotherhood, joy, Love, hope, faith, and undying devotion to truth and His way. For in bravery we must take these steps. Together we will go, trusting that the path shall be enlightened by His Love and our faith.

True Love is what this quest is for — true Love that can open hearts, dry tears, give hope of a new and better world and existence for ourselves and our children. Bring them up to know that God is present in all things at all times, that His Love is offered on all levels. We have but to acknowledge and accept it. And this world shall once again be a beautiful place in which to live, in which to love.

Shalom

VII

JOY

*J*oy comes from the heart. Joy is that feeling that comes from the connection to our source, our Father-Mother God. Joy is that Love that we feel when we are at one with Him, not experiencing that separation that has become man's usual state. The goal is to feel this connection, this joy permanently, not inconsistently.

Most experience what they believe to be joy in things that, in truth, do not produce true, everlasting joy. Shall we give you an example? The joy that is felt from the satisfaction from material gain. This and other examples like it are a transitory joy, a joy that is not everlasting, not a true joy. True joy will be felt in the heart and throughout the whole being on every level. True joy does not fade, but extends out through the aura and affects all those who come in contact with you.

Others are drawn to a soul who is exuding this joy. They may not even be aware of the source of this attraction. Yet it is strong, like a magnet. The Love of our Father-Mother God is the source of this joy. This joy can turn your life around, can lighten up any situation, any experience. For in knowing His Love and this true joy, all things are put in perspective. The perfection of the universe becomes truly known to the heart that is experiencing true joy. When others observe one who is blessed with true joy, they desire to experience this joy also. For true happiness stems from this joy. This joy makes life clear and beautiful.

Share the secrets of your joy with others. So many long for this joy, for this Love, within their hearts. So many are lost, unhappy, confused. Joy to them is a fleeting emotion that has no basis, no true foundation in their lives. What must be understood is that God is the source of all. He is our foundation, the basis of all that is. Through Him and His Love, one can know true Love, true joy, true happiness.

Man yearns for this knowledge. Man yearns for an end to the lifetimes and lifetimes of separation that he has been experiencing. He yearns for someone to show him the way. If you know and experience this joy, are an example of this true way of existence, don't keep secret your knowledge of joy and how to attain it. Share your experiences, share your joy. For now is the time in the Earth for all to become joyful once again, for true joy to be known, to be experienced, to be shared in our Father's Love. This is His wish: to see His children truly joyful, truly loving, truly at peace.

For the true basis of peace is joy. If one is joyful, in connection with the oneness of all life, at one with

the Creator, there is peace in his heart. If there is
peace within, that peace becomes manifested without
in the world around you. For in reality, this world is
but a reflection of what is within so many hearts.

Fear, anger, greed, and hatred are rampant upon the
Earth. This sadness, this pain, this grief must come to
an end. The true joy of oneness must once more be
experienced to make the changes desired on this planet. Each one of us must play our part in this healing.

The natural forces are also a part of this healing.
Floods, famine, drought, all types of natural disasters play their part in the healing of the Earth, of the
pulling together of the peoples of the Earth in Love
and in brotherhood. Pain, sickness, death, and ter-
ror must be experienced by many before the error of
their ways becomes apparent to them.

This is not what our Father wants for His children,
but it is what they have chosen. And as we are His co-
creators, He will not interfere except to send His armies
forth, His workers in the light, in the hopes of open-
ing man's eyes, man's spiritual eyes, to begin to see the
true essence, the true meaning of life. And that is joy,
joy and Love: the joy that results from the true Love of
God, true dedication and service to the path of Love —
Love of self and of all of our brothers and sisters.

A return to this path will be effected as a result of
all these disasters, as man opens his spiritual eyes
and eventually his heart to accept the Love which is
being offered, the true joy that is rightfully ours to
know and to experience.

We can affect these events. The more children of the light working together to change the consciousness on this Earth, the less will this pain and suffering be needed to effect the changes. Some of these changes can and will be effected peacefully. By acknowledging and extending the Love, the joy, and the peace within, these things will be known and manifested without in the world around us.

To do your part, start within and then make it your intent to extend the Love within as a loving hand to all those you meet in Love, in compassion, and in brotherhood, non-judgmentally and with true joy — the joy of knowing that we are all one. We are all His children, created equally out of Love and in Love.

All of creation is an energy. That energy is Love. Many veils have been covering this truth. It is now time to remove these veils, sometimes one by one, by each small act of kindness and Love, to finally unveil the truth of our oneness, the true purpose of our existence here on Earth and on every plane in existence — that of Love.

And joy will be the result of this return to oneness and to Love. And we shall live the lives that we are meant to live: those of peace, good will, happiness, and true joy. And He shall look with eyes of joy, smiling and laughing and relieved that His children are finally remembering the true meaning of life, their true heritage — that of joy, that of Love.

Shalom

VIII

PATIENCE

atience is that ability to truly live in the moment without concern for what will occur in the future. If you can truly do this, you are blessed with patience — the knowledge that all things happen in the proper time, in the perfect way. As one knows this truth, patience is the natural result. There is no need to work for this virtue. It is the natural outcome of faith in the perfection of the universe.

There is no future, only the now. If you are truly living in the moment, there is no concern for tomorrow and thus no need for patience. Patience is simply that ability to truly live in the moment, trusting that all things are unfolding as they should, according to divine plan. If all His children were more aware of this truth — the truth that all is perfect in this moment and forever — much hasty, incorrect action would be avoided. One would flow with life rather than fighting against the natural flow, natural progression of events.

Rejoice in the truth that patience is not something one need work for, but a gift to one's self through knowing and living the truth of perfection in the universe, faith in this perfection and in God. For all things shall come in their proper time. Fight not against self by interfering in the natural progression of events that are contributing to your growth, your knowledge. Accept life as it unfolds to you, and you will have no need for patience.

Patience is the natural outcome of true faith in self, in God, and in the perfection of the universe. Our desires to go against the natural flow of life lead many of us to action that is not conducive to peace, to harmony, to happiness. Your reality is the result of your thoughts — the builder, the blueprint of your life.

Your Higher Self and your God know what is proper for your growth and the proper unfoldment of events for your best interests. Know this truth and live this truth, and a peace will descend upon your life and the events in it. There will be no need to force results, to force events before their time. Impatience is simply not accepting that all is perfect here and now.

Patience shall be yours as the result of faith in the true path. Live in the moment. For if one is concerned always with what shall be, the majesty, the truth, and the experience of the moment are lost in useless frustration over what one desires instead of appreciation for what actually is. Plant the seeds for future events with your thoughts, with your prayers, and have faith that those events that shall contribute to that outcome will occur at the proper time, in the proper way. All shall come to pass as is judged best by your own Higher Self.

So know that by loving self, honoring self, honoring the truth of universal perfection, faith in that perfection and in God shall result in a mind and spirit which is patient, loving, and faithful. These attributes shall contribute greatly to your joy, to your ability to live your life to the fullest, in patience and in Love.

Shalom

IX

SEXUALITY

AND

SPIRITUALITY

*Y*ou have asked about sexuality and spirituality. They are not mutually exclusive. Sexuality is an energy, a universal energy, which has very good, very important purpose on the Earth, obviously. But besides procreation for man, it can be a completion, a unification of energies for very good, very spiritual purpose.

Making love between a man and a woman, or whichever genders choose to experience this activity together, is just what it says — making Love. It is a blending of God's energies on all levels. Think not that the physical act of making love is an activity that affects only the physical. This activity affects each person participating on all levels — physical, mental, emotional, and spiritual.

On one level, it is man's attempt to re-experience that unity from whence we came, that divine oneness with our Creator. For the energy that is experienced in that oneness with God is not unlike the ecstasy which is experienced on all levels through the physical act of making love.

When two people have chosen, out of Love and in Love, to blend their energies in this manner, it is a completion of sorts, a unity that reminds us of that unity that we all long for with God. We know not why we yearn so much for this completion, this joy. It is because of our separation. The physical act of making love is one way of recapturing, of recreating this unity, if only briefly, fleetingly.

God has no desire for man, to become spiritual, to put an end to this activity for purposes other than procreation. Sexuality is a part of life, a very beautiful part of life, and an expression of Love. Do not believe that to be a spiritual being, one must be celibate. This is a matter of choice. Some choose to expend this universal energy in other ways, to channel this creative energy into other activities. For what is sexuality but the energy of creation? The choice is yours. As His co-creator, you have the freedom to channel this creative energy in whatever manner you choose.

There have been created many fears concerning this energy. This energy is greatly misunderstood, greatly misused. It needn't be dealt with in fear and superstition. As always, if you will follow what feels right in your heart for yourself and no other, in each situation, you will choose to deal with this energy in a way which is appropriate for you.

At best, it is a declaration of Love, a creative energy expressed in a most beautiful way with benefit to those involved, a blending of energies on all levels in beauty and in joy, an expression of man's unity with God and the joy and Love that are experienced and created in that unity. At worst, it is a misuse of energy, creating *dis*-ease on all levels for those involved.

We are not here to make moral judgments regarding this activity. For all decisions must be made within thine own heart. And all those in touch with themselves, their God, and their purpose will know the proper use of this beautiful, creative energy.

So know that in His Love, God would wish that all His children find the expression of this energy and the use of this energy to be fulfilling and enlightening, an energy which is used not only to create the miracle of life, but to also create joy, Love, and wholeness — an energy which contributes to one's spirituality, Love of God, Love of self, and Love for and with another.

Know that the answers lie within thine own heart, in your wisdom and in your Love. Ask self and ask God for guidance concerning this matter and have faith that the answers will be made known within your heart and mind.

Shalom

X

THE LAW
OF SELF

*T*he Law of Self simply states that self is to be loved and honored as is thy neighbor, thy brother or sister. Choose to truly love and honor self, and yours will be a full cup from which to give. Constantly giving to others to one's own detriment makes for great difficulty in maintaining balance in one's life. Many choose the path of self-sacrifice. And yes, that path can and will lead to spiritual growth in some cases. And yet for so many who have lived many lifetimes of self-sacrifice, their path is one of honoring and loving self.

Many are confused concerning this law. It has been stated, "Love thy neighbor as thyself." It is important to note that it has not been stated, "Love thy neighbor *more* than self." For no one gains from the detriment of another. To truly give a gift that is beneficial to another, it needs to be given without cost to the giver.

Clarity of purpose is needed to truly understand this law. Is it God's wish that one would lay down his life for another, would give up his own purposes, his own desires, goals, and path so that another may profit? As always, the choice is the individual's. But many have lived many lifetimes with the false belief that another entity's purposes, dreams, and desires are more important than their own.

To truly be a chalice of Love and of light for thy brothers and sisters, one must first love self, honor self, fulfill those needs which contribute to one's own growth and purpose. As one's life is abundant on all levels, then that abundance may be shared with all whom one cares to share. Yes, you are your brother's keeper, but this need not be to your own detriment. One cannot give from an empty cup. One cannot truly feel the joy, the Love of brother-hood if he has not fulfilled the purposes of his own journey here on Earth.

Now one may say that perhaps one's purpose is to lay down his life for another. And this may be very true. Through a karmic debt or opportunity, some souls choose such paths. But many souls mistakenly believe that self is less important, less honorable than another and constantly deny their own fulfill-ment on one or many levels in favor of another's de-sires. This can lead to great suffering and can actually be an impediment to true spiritual growth.

While it is honorable and desirable to love thy neighbor as thyself, placing them neither above nor below self, one must love and honor self to achieve true freedom and oneness with God. One may serve God without depriving self. One may enjoy fulfillment, abundance on all levels without the need for sacrifice. For in truth, one must experience the joy of self-fulfillment of his own purposes to truly serve God. One should give from his own abundance, joy, and Love which has been achieved through honoring and loving self.

So do not believe that one must give up wealth, comfort, or joy to attain spiritual growth. For it is in achieving those things which lead to fulfillment of self that one has the freedom, the abundance from which to share in an attitude of generosity and lack of need.

One may not truly benefit at the expense of his brother's loss. Realizing that may help one to quicken his own spiritual growth. Love thy neighbor as thyself, not more than self. For you are also a precious child of God, with purpose and goals to be achieved which are of great importance. Know this truth, and do not place another's needs above thine own.

Parents, do not allow your children's needs to always take precedence. You should be the example of a fulfilling, rewarding life. And if your needs and desires are not met, you are not that example. In this example, of course, a balance must be achieved between fulfilling what is truly necessary for the child's well being and fulfilling the needs of self.

If one truly honors and fulfills the needs of self, one's cup will be overflowing with the nectar of Love, enough to nourish many others. If thy cup is constantly depleted, with no supply of nourishment being replenished, both self and those who have become dependent upon that well may die of thirst. Many believe that through their suffering, their lack, a great spiritual healing may take place. And in some cases this may be true. But most gifts of Love and joy are not given from a heart lacking in these.

The Law of Self simply is the universal law that to be of true service to another, one must first love and honor self. One of the greatest gifts one can give another is through living a life which is an example of abundance in all things that are truly important — Love, joy, peace, harmony, and freedom.

Begin within self, achieving those things which contribute to self and thus to others. Do not believe that thine own poverty on any level is contributive to another's joy. For on some level, one will always feel cheated if he constantly gives of self until there is nothing left to give. Know that to be a true channel of Love and of His light, one must love himself, honoring his own needs and purposes as important as any other's.

Fill thine own cup with Love, with abundance in all things, and then know the joy of being the wellspring from which others enjoy enrichment and nourishment. Constantly replenish the source of nourishment through loving God and loving self. As your needs are fulfilled, the greater your ability to be of service to others.

Shalom

XI

FORGIVENESS

orgiveness is that act that shall set you free. Forgiveness is a necessity if one is to live a life truly in harmony with his Higher Self and God. Forgiveness is the ability to truly see one's self at one with our brothers and sisters. For if we are all one and mirror each other, how can we help but forgive our neighbor in Love for all acts, all choices made that may affect us?

The place to begin is within self. To truly love yourself, begin with forgiving all those transgressions which are weighing heavily upon your heart — those transgressions which you have adjudged yourself to be guilty of, and those which have been perpetrated by others. Clear your heart of these burdens to truly begin to live your life honoring self, loving self.

Forgiveness is one of the keys to freedom. If you can truly love self through forgiveness of those burdens, those guilts, which weigh heavily upon your heart, then the path of forgiveness of others is much clearer, much more easily followed.

Forgiveness is the ability to truly be able to place yourself in your brothers' or sisters' footsteps and realize that their mistakes, their choices — which you have adjudged to have been a personal affront to self — are a part of the path that has led to growth, to understanding for one or both.

The greatest growth can be achieved through forgiveness, knowing that we are all one, that we have all made mistakes upon our paths, knowing and feeling the Love that is needed to truly apply the principles of Love and forgiveness. Each mistake or error, each step upon the path which is not in harmony with one's Higher Self, can lead to growth through the realization that different action may be needed if a similar situation arises. We have many lessons to learn here in this great classroom Earth.

Guilt is one of the biggest burdens one may bear. Guilt has no place in a heart that truly loves self. For to truly love self, we must accept that the mistakes, the errors upon our path are a necessary part of growth, a necessary step towards the light. Accepting our perfection, even in our blunders, is a necessary part of self-Love. And through this self-Love, one is truly able to love his fellow man, to accept his humanness.

There is great purpose to even those acts which seem the most heinous on this Earth. Forgiving another is a part of accepting that each event is part of the perfection of this universe and has good purpose, even if just to provide one the opportunity of forgiveness.

One who is truly seeking to know God and to love God will make it his intent to see the perfection of the universe, to see his oneness with each and every fellow man, to help that fellow man in whatever way possible upon his path. And that help may well be the simple act of forgiveness.

"Simple?" you ask. Forgiveness may not be a simple matter for one who has not learned to forgive self, has not accepted past action as a necessary part of growth. Begin within, and the forgiveness of others will become much easier, a natural result of the Love and forgiveness one affords self.

Forgiveness will lift years of sadness, of grief, of burden from thy heart. The freedom that is felt as a result of the act of forgiveness of self or another is a wondrous feeling. The removal of the burden frees one to achieve all manner of work and to experience great joy.

If you feel you have been wronged, confront the one you feel has wronged you. Try to put yourself into his shoes, so to speak, to truly try to see the situation from his perspective. Have you never acted in a similar manner? Chances are, the answer will be yes. And if it is yes, did you forgive self? If so, how can you fail to forgive your brother or sister who is just a part of thee? And if you have not forgiven self, why not? Aren't you aware that you are a beautiful child of God, deserving of your own forgiveness?

See your perfection in your imperfection, knowing that every "wrong" choice may not be wrong, but a step upon the path of growth and development needed by thy soul on its journey to oneness and the return to wholeness.

God does not keep a tally of thy mistakes, thy transgressions. God forgives one and all. Self is the one you need to ask for forgiveness. Self is the one who will stand in your own path of joy demanding perfection. Know that these transgressions are an important part of that path to enlightenment.

Love self and forgive self, acknowledging and granting that Love that is already offered from our Father-Mother God. You only have self to answer to. You are your own judge and jury, and more often than not, your own worst enemy. If you grant not self the Love you deserve, you will not be able to accept that Love which He offers with an open, forgiving heart.

Forgive self and feel the peace, the joy, and the freedom that results. See the light grow brighter within self and along the path which leads to true joy. And then extend this Love, this forgiveness to all those whom you meet in the new understanding, the new freedom you have gained through releasing the burdens of guilt through forgiveness. Let forgiveness rule thy heart and thy actions, and you will find you have moved by great leaps and bounds upon that path to oneness with God.

We hope that you shall accept the Love and for-

giveness that is always offered thee by thy Father-
Mother God, and that through this acceptance, that
Love and forgiveness will be extended to all those
you meet. As we look with eyes of Love upon ourselves and upon each other, this planet will begin to
radiate the Love which is extended to ourselves and
to our brothers and sisters. And we shall experience
a rebirth of hope, of joy, and freedom through this
Love.

Shalom

"May Peace Be With You
Now and Forevermore."

Mathias